AL'S TEN FINGERS

He Used Them To Play Music

Albert "Al" V. Martin

&

Sandra L. Winborne, Ph.D.

AL'S TEN FINGERS

He Used Them To Play Music

Albert "Al" V. Martin

&

Sandra L. Winborne, Ph.D.

.

Carter J. Gaston
Illustrator

DK1 Productions
Graphic Design

DEDICATION

Al dedicates his book to say thank you to his parents, Alvin and Annie Martin, who listened to him and bought him a piano and organ to practice playing music. Doing that, he was able to play for his church, starting at 12 years of age. Al also dedicates the book to his two children, Anna Michelle Martin, and Allen Matthew Martin! Al's message to them, "I always want you both to take pride in your gifts from God. Please use your talents to bring joy to the world. I love you!"

ACKNOWLEDGEMENTS

We sincerely thank all who provided your critical eyes, words of encouragement and guidance in self-publishing. We kindly thank LaVender Shedrick Williams, the owner and founder of Candy Publishing, who guided us through Amazon Kindle Direct Publishing (KDP). This book is a first, and therefore, we learned, we tried, and we completed *Al's Ten Fingers: He used them to play music.*

Al Martin was eight, and his sister, Marietta was five. She got a toy piano, and Al got a basketball for Christmas. Marietta did not like the toy piano, but Al did! He tried to play on the toy piano. Al always knew he wanted to use his ten fingers to play music. It made him happy to figure out how to make music.

Alvin and Annie Martin, Al's parents wanted their son to play a musical instrument. They chose a cornet for him. A cornet is like a small trumpet. Al was 10-years old, and the band director at Ransom High School, Mr. John Beck, asked Al's parents if he could play in the Ransom High School Marching Band. They said yes, and Al, along with his friend, Claude Smith, was small, but they played music with much older band members.

Al loved to play music and only music. Basketball, football, or any outdoor sports he liked but not as well as playing music. So, one day, Al went to his parents, took a deep breath, locked his fingers together, and asked his parents for a piano. They listened to him and said yes! It was for his 12th birthday, and Al promised his parents that he would learn how to play the piano in six-months.

Al kept his promise to his parents. He practiced the piano for four hours every day. While his brothers, sisters, and friends played outside; he played music on the piano.

Three months after Al received his piano, he played for the first time at his church. His parents were very proud. It took place at St. Peters Baptist Church at a Sunday morning worship service. Al continued to play for his church, and when the other musicians could not play, he did!

One day Al went to his mother and finding courage; he asked her to buy an organ. His mother thought about it and agreed with him. She worked with Mr. Ken Forbes, the owner of Forbes Music, Incorporated. She told Mr. Forbes that she would buy an organ for Al, only if he would teach her son how to play.

Mr. Forbes taught Al for only two weeks before he needed to find another organ teacher for him. Al practiced playing his organ for hours every night. He learned so fast, and soon, he knew how to play better than his teacher.

Al's new music teacher was Mrs. Emily Alderman. She was a teacher who taught students daily. On Saturday afternoons, she taught Al and two other students organ and piano.

The children from Al's church wanted him to teach them how to play the piano. So, he taught them! Al enjoyed teaching other children how to play. He used the church's piano for the children's lessons.

Al continued learning from Mrs. Alderman how to play the piano and organ. For three years, he took lessons. When he was 15 years old, he played his first organ recital at St. Peters Baptist Church, on Kershaw Street in Pensacola, FL. It was for the church's Christmas concert and announced in *The Pensacola News Journal*.

Al Martin knew he wanted to play piano and later the organ since he was a little boy. Sometimes children see that they want to play music. Maybe if they tell their parents as Al did, they may get an instrument to learn how to play.

Today, Al Martin is a full-time career musician. He has played music in New York and Georgia. Currently, Al teaches music lessons at Blues Angel Music. He also plays on a grand piano at Jeweler's Trade Shop, in downtown Pensacola, and he plays piano or organ at Greater Union Baptist Church. Two repeating piano performances took place at the Backyard at The Space and The District Seville Steak and Seafood Restaurant. Al enjoys playing gospel, jazz, show tunes, and many other types of music. You can hear him play beautiful music around the City of Pensacola.

What are you doing with your ten fingers? Do you want to be like, Al, and play piano and organ? Or do you want to learn how to play another type of musical instrument? Learning to play music may help you learn many other things in school and life.

You Can Try Music!
What instrument will you try? Who will teach you?

Musical Instruments _____

Instructor _____
Phone _____
E-mail _____

Instructor _____
Phone _____
E-mail _____

Instructor _____
Phone _____
E-mail _____

Instructor _____
Phone _____
E-mail _____

NOTES

Meet the Authors

Albert "Al" V. Martin

Mr. Al Martin has been playing piano since 1963. A few years later, he started playing the organ, still a child with a gift from God. Al has taught at music stores (currently Blues Angel Music), churches, after-school programs, and private homes. He studied music at Pensacola Junior (State) College and Berklee College of Music in Boston, MA. He played music in New York and Atlanta. He still plays music today. Mr. Albert V. Martin's Contact: pianamart@yahoo.com or (850) 982-7935

Sandra L. Winborne, Ph.D.

Dr. Sandra Winborne, aka, Sandy, is an educator who retired in December 2014 from the United States Department of Navy, after over 28-years of service. She has an education consultant business called Winnie & Associates, LLC. Winborne is also a singer of gospel, jazz, standards, show tunes, and classically trained in Upstate New York. Winborne is currently writing Mr. Al Martin's Adult Book, and the proposed title is "Talent Over Adversity." Contact: drwinborne@gmail.com or (850) 206-4814.

Made in the USA
Columbia, SC
20 August 2020

16962452R00020